THE CALCULUS
OF FALLING
BODIES

THE CALCULUS
OF FALLING
BODIES

POEMS

GEOFF RIPS

San Antonio, Texas

2015

The Calculus of Falling Bodies © 2015 by Geoff Rips

Cover art: Angel from Scrovegni Chapel, Giotto's "Lamentation"

First Edition

Paperback original ISBN-13: 978-1-60940-419-2
Ebooks:
ePub ISBN: 978-1-60940-420-8
Kindle ISBN: 978-1-60940-421-5
Library PDF ISBN: 978-1-60940-422-2

Wings Press
627 E. Guenther
San Antonio, Texas 78210
Phone/fax: (210) 271-7805

On-line catalogue and ordering:
www.wingspress.com
All Wings Press titles are distributed to the trade by
Independent Publishers Group
www.ipgbook.com

Library of Congress Cataloging-in-Publication Data:

Rips, Geoffrey.
  [Poems. Selections]
  The calculus of falling bodies : poems / Geoff Rips. -- First edition.
    pages ; cm
  ISBN 978-1-60940-419-2 (softcover : acid-free paper) -- ISBN 978-1-60940-420-8
(epub ebook) -- ISBN 978-1-60940-421-5 (kindle-mobipocket ebook) -- ISBN 978-
1-60940-422-2 (library pdf ebook)
  I. Title.
  PS3618.I67A6 2015
  811'.6--dc23

                        2014039245

CONTENTS

THE CALCULUS OF FALLING BODIES

In memory of my father
& for my mother

As in all things,
for
Nancy
Gabriela
Sascha

POETRY, JOURNALISM, WRITING, THE WORLD

The spring is not cowled so deeply under the hill
that the water is brilliant and nervy, seeming to break
in the mouth like crystals, as spring water can:
it is about the temper of faucet water, and tastes slack
and faintly sad, as if just short of stale.
It is not quite tepid, however,
and it does not seem to taste of sweat and sickness,
as the water does which the Woods family have to use.

—*Let Us Now Praise Famous Men*
James Agee [line breaks added]

You might want to talk about the relationship between your journalism and your poetry, Bryce Milligan suggested when he accepted my poetry for publication by Wings Press. After all, he said, more people know you as a journalist (a very small universe to begin with) than as a poet. How do those fit together?

I tried to remember what the elders had written about this. Three towering 20th century contemporaries, the American poets Ezra Pound, William Carlos Williams, and Archibald MacLeish, clearly thought about these things a great deal. Pound described literature as "news that STAYS news." From an open-air prison in Pisa, Italy, where he was held as an American prisoner for treason during World War II, Pound's "Pisan Cantos" are a report on the state of his own mind and on the world, ancient and contemporary. They are among his best works.

His old college pal, William Carlos Williams, a family doctor in Rutherford, New Jersey, wrote poems about red wheelbarrows and chickens but also a book-length poem on the history and life of Paterson, New Jersey. He also wrote a set of essays, *In the American Grain*, helping

XI

to define American character and re-orient American history. Williams wrote: "It is difficult to get the news from poems, yet men die miserably every day for lack of what is found there."

Finally, Archibald MacLeish, poet, lawyer, Pulitzer Prize winner, appointed Librarian of Congress and Undersecretary of State by FDR (a liberal Democrat who was instrumental in getting Pound freed from St. Elizabeth's mental hospital, where he had been imprisoned for 13 years), wrote: "Call a book *Das Kapital* or *The Voyage of the Beagle* or *Theory of Relativity* or *Alice in Wonderland* or *Moby Dick*, ... it is still a 'report' upon the 'mystery of things.'"

Why else write?

My father was a poet. He worked in the family business selling water-well pipe and kept a small notebook in his pocket, where he jotted down lines to use later in poems. He encouraged day dreaming. Because it was valued in my home, I did a lot of that. As a kid, I remember lying on my bed, looking out the window, listening to the banana leaves brush the screen and thinking about "the mystery of things." On Sunday mornings, we listened to poets reading their works on Caedmon Records. Even when I didn't understand what they were saying, the cadences and rhythms of Robert Frost, MacLeish, T.S. Eliot and Randall Jarrell worked their way into my blood. Writing poetry, then, became a natural way in my boyhood home to express myself and to try to understand the world. I went on to study writing with poet Richard Wilbur at Wesleyan University and continued my formal education with poet Ruth Stone in graduate school at Indiana University. Ruth helped me understand the importance of meaning in poetry. Later visits to her battered home in the woods of Vermont were like entering an oasis of language.

But, as a child of the '60s, I thought it necessary to help change the world (and still do). Through the American Friends Service Committee in San Antonio, I began writing a few pieces for an anti-war underground newspaper, the *Eagle Bone Whistle*. While teaching English in the night school of St. Philip's College in San Antonio and writing poetry, I wrote a novel, hoping to understand San Antonio in a way that William Carlos Williams showed us Paterson. I was your typical over-reaching young writer. But I had decided that San Antonio could be best revealed in fiction rather than poetry or through New Journalism.

A few years later, while living in New York City, I edited a newsletter on repression in Latin America, created by Latin American political refugees. Then I became an editor for *Punto de Contacto/Point of Contact,* a journal of arts and politics in Spanish and English, produced by a community of Latin American exiles. Art critic Dore Ashton, who worked closely with these Latin American exiles, arranged for PEN American Center to hire me to write a report on government suppression of underground newspapers in the United States. The foundation of this report would be extensive files obtained through the Freedom of Information Act and housed in Allen Ginsberg's Lower East Side apartment. A high point of my life was sharing three-minute eggs with Allen and Peter Orlovsky before going through the files, which more than once produced what Allen called "the smoking typewriter," showing government sponsorship of illegal attacks on underground newspapers and their staffs. Allen later saw to it that this was published as *UnAmerican Activities* by City Lights Books. Then PEN hired me to run its human rights program protesting censorship and the imprisonment of writers around the world. I kept writing poetry and began writing a few magazine articles.

One of these was on the vein of populism still running through parts of rural Texas. It was published in *The Texas Observer.* Not long after, I became associate editor, then editor of the *Observer,* writing my heart out about politics, society, related skullduggery, the arts, and the landscape of Texas. Some of these same things appeared in my poems, but as McLuhan said, the medium shaped the message, another way of applying quantum theory's dictum that how you measure determines what gets measured and what gets reported.

And so mine has been a writing life. Not a life of talk shows and book tours, but a writing life nonetheless. My novel, *The Truth* (New Issues, 2008), won a national writing prize. I'm working on another novel, a number of articles, a few poems, book reviews, and a blog. To earn a living, I write speeches, grant proposals, position papers, and scripts for public events. Writing fiction is always good preparation for writing grant

XIII

proposals. The distinctions on the creative side blur, just as the reporting by James Agee at the beginning of this introduction becomes a poem when the line breaks are added. Dante's *Divine Comedy* and Chaucer's *Canterbury Tales* are the best reporting we have on the customs, politics, and social mores of their worlds, while allowing us to see into the souls of individual people inhabiting those worlds. The same with newspaper editor Walt Whitman's reporting on mid-19th century America in his epic poem, "Song of Myself."

All of which is to say that the first reason I write is to find out what I'm thinking. The second reason is to convey this understanding to others, hoping it will prove useful to them. I'm fortunate to have several ways to get there. The form and the subject choose me as much as I choose them. All this is in the service of better understanding "the mystery of things."

The poems in this collection span almost four decades. Undergirding all my writing is the profound and wonderful complication of family. I am grateful to Bryce Milligan and Wings Press for making this publication possible.

—GR
July 28, 2014

COMPOST

COMPOST

for Gabriela

Grapefruit rind, onions' outer skin, pliant celery stalks, lemon gone
soft and gray underneath, what's left of what was used for soup
last night and what was salvaged from the refrigerator bin, all hauled
in a bucket by my daughter, poured into the darkening moist leaves,
turning to black, wet ur-matter, breaking down to the basics,
worms, pillbugs, bacteria eating and churning the arrogance of finely
    hewn form
—a maple leaf, for instance—until it can't be recognized, until
it can't be separated from the rest of the agglomeration of life, what
    comes before
and what comes after, what is living in single-celled simplicity,
what once lived, what will live again. Leaves and celery stalks
straining toward the only immortality that awaits us, turnips and beauticians,
providing fodder for our children and generations of children
and hogs and cucumbers and bacteria to come, so that they take us in,
turn us back to what we came from, our community of amino acids, our
    compost,
these singular forms just a passing fancy, a dance, a flourish,
while the real work of the world goes on here, not an arm's length
from my beautiful daughter's delicate hand, death churning itself into life,
the used-up not all used up, the carcass aglow, the spent husk served
as banquet for more life, bacteria feasting, the whole more driven
than its parts to survive. And the rest of it—people, lettuce, cows—
just aberrations to be tolerated, grist for the mill, fodder for the machine,
to keep it turning, generating heat at its center, the combustion of decay.

2

Feel the heat, I tell my daughter. She sticks a spindly arm into the center
        of the heap, then
draws it back. Nice and warm, I say. Slimy, she replies,
turning in her purple dress and skipping away, past the peach tree.
Oh, how singular. How pristine. How I held her, pulled
from the center of her mother, bright-eyed, fur gleaming, wet. She looked me
in the eyes, as if to say, I understand all this already—let's move on. Skipping
down the hill, she has paid homage to decay and now is turning
        cartwheels in the grass.
I turn to follow. How to consider this set against the cold stars?
The conceit of churning and returning. The empire of bacteria.
Chemical reactions. No real reason for it, except that it's work to do.
Orange rind, elm leaf, earthworm, the turn of my daughter's hand,
generating heat, generating heat at the heart of it all.

DOLPHIN

for Sascha

My younger daughter, who is six, can stand
in the middle of the backyard, a field, the universe,
and take it all in. This still small girl with large hands.
This summer we sat for long stretches on the rocks of a jetty
and watched bottle-nosed dolphin in pairs
drawing their perfect arcs among the choppy waves of the channel.
Sometimes they came within twenty yards of where we sat.
One smiled at me, my daughter said, squatting on the rocks,
chin in her hands. She was not surprised;
she was pleased, thoughtful, feeling part of this world,
the water sloshing among the rocks of the jetty, all of it,
the sun going down, the breeze constant, smelling of bait
that fishermen had left on the jetty, the shrimp boats
ferrying by, followed by clouds of gulls calling to empty nets,
the Norwegian freighter slipping almost silently through the breach,
one man standing on the long, barren deck, staring past us, down the coastline,
the ship's wake reaching us minutes later, rolling into the rocks,
splashing our knees. All of it.
Not far from here, five years ago, nearly three hundred dolphin
beached, belly up, covered with a fungus.
Such news has yet to reach my thoughtful young daughter,
now resting on her haunches on the rocks,
looking for dolphin, calculating the world.

4

WETLANDS

for Gabriela

So much of the world is floating.
The timeless dive of Kemp's Ridley sea turtle,
spiraling down, down in the deep green sea,
schools of amberjack gliding patiently
among the steel legs of oil rigs,
ling, sleek and unperturbed,
nurse shark hugging the bottom of the Gulf,
cruising two inches above the grit
of the ocean floor. Ponderous jewfish, not moving, waiting
to eat whatever the currents bring,
growing fat, huge, timeless,
missing the hormone that limits growth, a naturalist
once explained. The ever-expanding universe
of the self, hovering above the Gulf floor.
My pre-adolescent daughter asked just the other night
what hormones are. You don't want to know, we said.
They limit growth, we'd wanted to say.
But we'd be wrong.

Cormorant, gray heron, sandhill crane extracting
one stilt from the grasses, then the other, moving forward
slowly, eyes always on the movement of the shallows
in this place not quite water, not quite land.
Brown pelican, waddling out of the Pleistocene,
but when it takes its ungainliness to the air,

it too is floating. Rowing on currents of air
over the marshes, where it stops,
folds its long wings, then drops like a javelin into the stillness,
to emerge again like an oiled spectre from another age,
rocking on the water for only a moment, then flapping to become airborne,
floating again above the grasses, sandbars, shallows, lagoon and us,
its wings outstretched, so little effort, so far outside time.
So much of the world is floating,
as I stand, landlocked, watching my daughter watch the pelican,
then leaping herself, *jeté* on the jetty,
then again, arms thrust to the skies, then again
and she's gone.

6

I LIFT HER UP

for Gabriela and Sascha

I.

Snow still on the mountains above Taos. My daughters
are growing older. We park in the center
of the pueblo, tourists by the Red Willow waters
rushing like stallions, filling the banks. We enter
the pueblo at its heart, where small red willows
dip just the tips of branches into the galloping maelstrom. They stand
by the rampaging chaos—its witness. Melting snows
and mountain storms in a churning rush to the Rio Grande.
My older daughter follows the tour guide closely, standing
by her as she speaks at cemetery, chapel, stream.
Our daughter is eager to learn. She worships the tour guide,
who explains that the dead are wrapped and piled as one unending
body, generations sinking into each other, erasing time,
ribs spiraling down, the humus of a people on fire inside.

II.

There was a fire here. The church, a sanctuary in more than name,
where women and children gathered, huddled against the onslaught
of the U.S. Cavalry. The Taos people would not concede the claim
on their world by an alien empire. Burned to the ground, the safety sought
found only in one another, in an eternal embrace of generations.
A sacred graveyard now, marked off by the broken adobe walls
of the old sacristy. Crosses at odd angles. Mounds of bodies—a nation's
past piled three, four, six feet high. Replenished as each old one falls
into his mother's arms. I wonder what my daughter
thinks about all this. The too palpable dead
where the Red Willow comes crashing. The play
in her mind unfolding, the ceaseless rush of waters
across an endless expanse of time. Families collapsed.
She won't walk with us today.

III.

My younger daughter is struggling to learn to swim. Soon
she will. She resolutely enters every motel swimming pool
but stiffens as I angle her body to meet the water's plane.
I lift her up. She trusts me and doesn't trust me. But I'm all
she's got in this uncertain water. She's secure on land:
ordering nachos, she's on her own, telling the patient waiter
which chile to leave off, which cheese to use. As if I'd planned
this brief, mundane nirvana, this space inhabited by daughters
of seven and ten, pristine, the rushing of Red Willow kept at bay
for a moment. I want to hold on, to bear-hug time.
I know what I have, but not how to hold it.
We're at the mercy of the onrushing waters. It's one thing to say,
Stand back. I try. But this is our moment in this expanse, our sublime
moment, the center of family unfolded.

RESUSCITATION

HALITOSIS
OR
I'M NOT SHERMAN AND YOU'RE NOT GEORGIA

When we kissed
death blew from your mouth
like a warm wind over Gettysburg.
I tasted blue- and gray-capped
bodies lying face to face,
row on row, fields of rotting wheat
and butchered hogs.
When we kissed
your death curled into mine
and our tongues
shook hands at Appomattox.

WHY I NEVER HAVE ANYTHING TO SAY TO YOU

Last week I went swimming
with no one I knew, only the yellow
wood light and the fish
that bumped me along. Returning
to my clothes, I found my shoes
had swallowed their tongues.

———•———

I now live in the back seat
of a green Ford coupe on the edge
of town. RFD. When the mailman comes,
I lock the doors and low
like a green Guernsey. The letters
he leaves from you I convert to milk.

———•———

Paris and the last time we were together
I was mad for the Rue de Rosiers:
the bagel-eyed French, the Yiddish
cafes. Here I could speak: "Challah,
Hamantaschen." But you were always tugging
the other way: your wet hair, patrician nose,
cold feet. You resented gefilte fish.
When your icy hand grabbed mine,
the lakes of New England froze over.

TRAFFIC

I'm late for work, idling now under a canopy of sycamores
where the runners have stopped on the curb, sweat
illuminating their flesh as they pace back and forth,
hands on hips or talking on cell phones, pulling
their hair back and wringing it out, twisting sweatbands,
unable to stand still, like horses nearing the starting gate, shifting
from one leg to the other, waiting for the light to change.
Why aren't they working? They take off at a trot, crossing
in front of me as I wait, late for a meeting that doesn't really matter.
Waiters, brokers, people who office at Starbucks,
trust fund babies, house flippers. Do they sing in the shower?
Are they still mulling remnants of last night's dreams?
Ear plugs set, tuned to their own music, the runners don't hear
what the world has to say, that the imagination founders
as you drive to work or simply wait, engine thrumming, for them to cross.

Hours later in our room in our bed, our knowing feet
rub past each other. Traffic shows us our place
in the world, dictates the pace of our being. I think of this
as you turn toward me, your book falling to the sheet.
When you leave for work, the traffic seems to carry you
away from this house, as if you are hoisted by hundreds of hands
above a mosh pit and ferried away. But what if we lived
on some great jungle river where the days did not lead one
to the next but were the same day lived over

and over again with slight variations in the heat and the showers
among tapirs and savage fish? That kind of traffic,
where the going carried you forward then carried you back.
The same day every day. You turn out the light. I enter
the slipstream. My hand inches toward the intersection
of your left leg and your right, waiting for the light to change.

MOWING IN THE DARK

for Nancy

The fall sun sets so soon. I rattle the mower
out of the garage, pull the cord in the yellow blaze
of last light, and take off around the yard.
Mowing by moonlight, by memory and feel,
by streetlight in the side yard, riding
the familiar undulations of the ground.
And when morning comes, I can't wait
to walk out into the wet, cut green,
to see the tiny rills and hedgerows of my going,
the tufts missed in pockets of the earth,
the sensuous curves of grass in one direction and then another.
Here against the grain, and there along the nap.
Seeing where I've been. And where I have still to go.
The dark secrets of my mowing.

So when you lie in bed and say,
"Turn off the light,"
I'm ready.

16

EPOXY

There are cracks in the body of love.
We've been apart too long.
I'm leaking blood and hair.
The pavement knows me.
I'm seeping through my shoes.

There are cracks in the body of love.
Our statues look across a trail of sawdust.
Snails trace my tracks back and forth
through Arkansas and Tennessee.
Through Virginia and New Jersey.
They are sticking to the Holland Tunnel walls.
They move like glue. Methodically
they press their lips
to all the space between us.

There are cracks in the body of love.
I'm moving toward you now
bringing all I own to fill them:
sticks and gravel, mortar
and sawdust rescued in my pockets.
I'm coming to you
holding all I can.
I'm coming like a workman
baring all his skills.

I'm a week away.
I'm three days away.
I'm hammering at your doorstep.
I'm sealing off all the space behind me.

ST. MATTHEW'S PASSION

They're outside again, carrying each other
on their shoulders. He rides her
across the yard; she rides him back.
My neighbors know how to live.

I'm here inside carrying myself
back and forth across the room.
And you're probably still mad
because the last time we met
I failed to notice the air turn over.
Well, now that it's too late,
I thought you should know I've been awakened
in recent nights cooing and kissing
everything that has your face and smell.
I've found myself walking toward you in the dark,
singing through your name. Lately
I've slept with every corner of this house.
I thought you should know. The next time
you press your lips to walls, there will be certain walls
that are kissing back.

SOMETHING LARGER

What part of desire is loneliness? A sudden wind off the Gulf
sends the tall palms into a frenzy under an impeccably blue sky,
whipping the fronds so violently that all the swimmers around the pool
look up expecting to see the curled outer edge of a squall
but instead see nothing but blue, but also no gulls floating in the ether
as they had been all day. A ten-year-old boy gets out of the pool
and stands dripping facing the wind, letting it shut his eyes
and tug the baggy red swim trunks against his legs.
The high wind blowing through him. It doesn't lift him
but instead grabs him and sends him roller-blading
across the puddled cement patio, slamming into the brick wall
of the hotel bar and grill. Then it stops. The boy gets up, smiling,
seized by something larger than himself. He wipes his eyes,
takes a running start, and cannonballs into the water. Desire
expands the universe, as you might send a bottle of wine
across the room to a table you've longed to join,
the woman with long, dark hair throwing her head back
after sipping the wine you've proffered,
and the tall, darkly handsome man in white polo
and blue blazer gives you a sign, touching his forefinger to his brow,
thanking you for paying homage to their privilege from across the room
in a way that makes you feel as if you're standing in an aisle
at a Louisiana Walmart holding jugs of water as the store fills
with Lake Pontchartrain, and the woman with dark hair waves to you
from the deck of the Carnival cruise liner that makes one last pass
to view the wreckage before sailing out to sea.

APPEAL

Table set. Pot on stove. Tell me, what can we do
to make this go on? Tell me. Girls in their rooms.
One dressed in hat and boa, twirling
in front of her mirror, trying not to miss
a moment of herself. Tell me.
The other mixing jigsaw parts.
Refitting knobs and notches. Tell me.
Wine is poured. The children eating soup.
Life is short. And getting shorter every day.

The kids in bed. I make my rounds. Front door.
One child, a still life between two stuffed bears.
Mail on the table. Tell me. The other,
covers thrown off, frozen in full gait. Running.
Back door. Can something new come of this?
Tell me. The house is dark. The cat climbs a screen.
I sit on the couch listening. Can I hear you sleeping
in our bed? Tell me. The house shifts.
If I stand too quickly, will all this slide away?

AUBADE

for Nancy

It's all I can do to think. It's all I can do not to think.
It's all I can do to open my eyes in the morning, to turn
to my left, to see you lying there watching me,
to see you closing your eyes pretending to sleep.
"You always look at me as if I were dying," you told me.
"You look at people as if they were no longer alive."
You told me this, lying in your bed, our bed.
You told me this and I lay beside you watching,
waiting for you to cry. But you wouldn't cry.
Instead you turned to the window by our bed
and watched the trees or watched the sky.
I think you watched the sky.

RESUSCITATION

for Nancy

What day was it we first made love?
What day was it we finally got it right,
sailing out on each other's breath?
The rower and the water. I'm trying to remember
because today I realized what's important
about living in this city. It's the way
every time I breathe I take in air
that someone else has just let go.
All this air here swirled through
so many lives. So many lungs. Passed around.
All those windpipes. All those years of coughing,
clinging breath. I mean the way we take it in
and give it back. What must go on inside us.
What we make our own. All this constant
intercourse, this peopled air.
The way we make love sometimes:
I take you in, you take me in,
you feed me, I feed you.

23

PERSONAL GEOGRAPHY

A LANDSCAPE

The woman across the street leans out naked
every morning over her window box. The man
there wears a hair shirt. It looks that way
from here as he grabs her from behind
and lifts her breasts from the geraniums.
I turn around and around.
It is summer. It is winter.
The woman downstairs slams her doors.
She is slowly dying. She leaves
her spittle on the banister. It thickens
in cold weather and will not dry.

NEW YORK CITY, THE WAY IT IS

A woman walks across the street
leaning on three sticks. Two are in her left hand.
Another woman spends her days
riding subways looking through a viewmaster
at Cypress Gardens, Reno, other worlds.
What is it that I'm saying?
I could have said there is a moth
that drags its gray wings across the windowsill,
and when it flies, it drops straight down.
It came here from the floor above.
There are two floors left below me.
We fall into the way we live.
The man who washes windows in this building
has been crawling out on ledges
for more than forty years. His wife
sews patches on the knees of his coveralls.
He doesn't try to keep them clean.
No one complains, his wife least of all.
There are many ways to live inside a skin.
The way we live chooses us,
then we pull it on.

The pigeons here are white above,
all gray below, turning
in the near, blue sky.

AS I WAS SAYING

It's raining and I'd give anything to know why.
No deer in New York anymore. Is that what
they cry about in bars? No more deer.
They're probably all in the woods somewhere
munching apples with no desire for city life.
I don't know. Five times today I've run into my own shadow
going the other way. It wouldn't stop. It wouldn't
even act like it knew me. It just kept walking,
talking to itself. Down the street. Around the corner.
It bought a paper. Then it stepped into a doorway
and disappeared.

ODE TO THE LESSER AND GREATER COCKROACH

Brown fingernails of shame
that scramble through the pots
and pans at night,
last spots sliding from the edge of vision
when the kitchen light comes on,
you that skirt the mesa of my boot's temptation
like a stagecoach with the mailbags
of disaster from the East,
brown shells of eternal movement
that run inside my walking, walk
inside my sitting down, scurry through my sleep,
you whose nest was once a hairbrush
and whose lovebed is a drawer of socks,
whose children and whose children's children
become the fingers that dance inside a wall,
you who hunger like the dry bark
whose stomach is a rotten wood,
iron filings eating up the magnet of desire,
you who glide like splinters
through the pipes and across the desk,
you the shells of stale pecans
scrabbling in a world of bitter angles,
all of you moving faster than remorse:
I can't fight the lean and hungry look
that faces down eternity.

I suspect when struck your back of shale
splits into two more cockroaches.
Besides, I have yet to turn on the faucet
in the morning to be showered
by a stream of cockroaches,
though I soon expect it.

But you, fat steamship of the white cliffs
of my bathtub: this has gone on long enough.
All day I see your thin brown headlights
flashing from the drain.
And tonight when I found you resting
on the porcelain like a fat grape of despair,
like a gaping mouth of nothingness,
like the insides of the drainpipes,
it was all I could do not to wash you
back into that darkness forever.
But then again, maybe you were saying something,
fat seed that sometimes flies like a barn roof.
Maybe you were showing me the whiteness of the bathtub,
or the dark veins running through the house,
holding all of this together.

SURVIVAL

Something is wrong with the world.
The walls of the buildings are thicker today.
The bricks are fat. They sweat at every pore.
I don't know what it is. Boys play baseball
in a vacant lot and a crowd of thousands
rises with a single cry. A symphony
moves past me lugging its dead toward home.
Even the violins sink in the mud.
Everything is wrong today.
The fence across the street comes toward me.
The boys playing baseball take out leather straps
and beat the walls. I can't get out the door.
The fire escape is pressed against the window.
I walk to the kitchen and back.
Even my breath drags behind me.
It stops in the room I have left.
It waits for me to go on.
I go on, this room
to the next to the next,
trying to stay alive.

TONIGHT THE WORLD STARTED OVER

Tonight the world started over.
At 11 o'clock on a certain corner
it started over again.
It's nothing new. The world stops sometimes.
Then it begins again. The woman
with the umbrella always on that corner
always asking for money. Money for food,
she says. Tonight is no exception.
She doesn't know what she needs.
I don't know what to give her.
Money for food, she says.
It's reason enough. We are agreed.
The walk home tonight in the new world
is already becoming familiar.
I've walked this way before.
This new world is a refuge.
I've come home to myself again.
I think there are reasons for living.
There are reasons for almost everything.

LOOKING FOR WORK

Today I feel like someone
who is capable of doing something.
It won't last.
Soon they'll grab me and say,
"All the decisions are ours."
But today I feel capable of anything,
capable of rejecting myself,
capable of lying in the street,
capable of digging my own grave.

WORK

A man with the name Angel sewn on his shirt stands glumly
behind a checkout counter at the hardware store. His register is jammed.
Three or four of us standing in line shift from one foot to the other.
We toy with wing nuts on display and watch Angel angrily
because we're hungry and his register is jammed.
Angel is waiting for a manager to free him from this frozen instant
in the great river of commerce. He grips the sides of his register
as if they were the shoulders of a child and stares off above our heads
to the ceiling fan display and beyond. He must have family at home,
works two jobs probably, never quite sleeps enough.
The nature of work is so diminished.

When I think of work, I think of my immigrant grandfather and
        great uncle
pulling nails out of boards with their teeth. That was sport to them.
They elbowed their way through the railyards of Oklahoma, strapping
Russian Jews, pitting muscle against the dangers of the oilfields.
Or Fred Sims. I worked with him summers, giving him the chance
to swing I-beams within inches of my head to keep me in my place.
Did I almost hit you, honey? he asked one or two beats late in that
        high-pitched voice of his.
Fred Sims, who laid railroad track through the Rockies, talked of nights
        spent among mountain lions.
The dignity of pure labor. Of sweat.
His black arms at 70 as taut and lean and steely as a young middleweight's.

There are no standards to go by.
Work now means Angel standing sad-faced waiting for the register
          to unjam.
No measures. No depth. No wilderness inside us
that we work to wear down with hard labor.
Just the dull slide to oblivion.
No feral eyes tracking the night. No living on instinct.
No fox tiptoeing its way through the heart. No measure of us beyond
          ourselves.
Nothing left to tame.

MADRID 1974

for Neruda

Today I was reading certain poems
of yours in a bar in dark Madrid
when a crowd of students paraded by
demanding freedom for your Chile.
Even in this Spain.
You couldn't have separated them
with a knife, they were so tightly meshed,
but a woman in black cut through
with a loaf of bread. A man at the bar stood
at the door to watch them pass.
He didn't show what he was thinking.
The years had made him careful.
A few minutes after the students,
the police cars went by, their sirens
reaching into the bar. And the waiter
turned to the bartender and laughed.
He had no teeth. This is only to say

that even when the dead stop singing
there is a song sitting in the branches
even when there are no leaves.
Watch the birds in the plaza near evening.
Sometimes they leave off picking in the grass
and fly straight into a window
just for the hell of it.

36

FATA SUSANNA, DON'T YOU CRY

The blue moon sits behind the new moon.
What sad strength.
My father long ago resigned himself
to the end of the world. "It won't be premature,
just soon," he used to tell us. "I don't
worry about it for myself. It's fine with me.
But for the rest of you—I hope I'm wrong."
Ever since I can remember: standing always
in his khakis with a peach pit
under a live oak tree.
                              On the other hand,
I once heard a Chinese poet say,
"Breaking into spring everywhere hastens
my old age." I almost got it once, surrounded
by sixteen-year-old girls, their tongues lapping.
I almost got it. Not enough spring left to go around
though. The plaster crumbles, revealing
spider eggs and I-beams. Taxis cruise the Sinai
breaking into prophecy. A wilderness of lost fares.
The last wave of a hand from Tehran.

FACED WITH A STALLED ECONOMY,
THEY TRY TO BRING AN END TO WHAT WE KNOW

The clear, untroubled waters of America
where my friends Dan and Bill and Mike were almost killed
in 1974 in Georgia, near Albany, near Americus, not far
from Plains, by three white thugs, farmboys on barbiturates
in a pickup truck. Carried them into the woods
by a clear stream. Brought out knives, chains, handcuffs.
Mosquitoes and cool water. My friends barely saved
by the slow pulse of Phenobarbital in the veins
of the swamps of the South.

The clear, untroubled waters of America. Dan finally killed
four years later in Vermont. Ice cold streams
rushed around him. Driven wild, poor Dan.
Deer licked his brains.
                    Oh, the clear, untroubled waters.

And then went down to the ship. Bombs
for Afghanis. Guns to Iraq. Boys grown up
in deep Georgia. Loaded with purpose.
They make ready for war.

DREAMS

The subconscious of America is paper thin. No dreams to culture
in a petri dish. I'm rescued briefly by a rush of cedar waxwings
attacking the berry bush by the back door, a factory
of brown and yellow plundering the green world,
working through its honeycomb then lifting off as one,
like a helicopter rushing to a burn victim on the highway.
The beating flurry like life inside me, a wind
through the soul's cavity until the MTV video jock
turns to the model standing beside him on the cliff
above the California beach, the ocean pounding the rocks below.
She's waiting to eat worms on television before he grabs the wheel
on the steel cable that will sling him into the ocean and certain death
or onto a life raft and a million dollars. Our anorexic inner life.
We're standing in the creek of this nation's sins and the water's rising,
but we're waiting for the bronzed model in blue bikini
to come parachuting in with a casserole of churning beetles
to nourish our scavenging souls and make us forget
we're nothing inside. As our President
returned from vacation after our history's deadliest hurricane
to tell the press that he hadn't realized things were this bad
or he would have skipped trimming mesquite and riding his bike
for the cameras. But this is America, he said,
and America always rises to the top. Bouncing on a life raft
as we're carried out to sea. A quick wave
as he entered the helicopter. No more conviction
than the plastic trout mounted on the wall above the bartender

at the Lonesome Oak saloon, turning its head when you push a button
to say, What you lookin' at? while we try to claw our way out
of the primordial slime like lungfish pulling up into the air
to say simply, "The world is complex." Not what the crowd at Hooter's
wants to hear. Keep it simple. The dream of America
pulling out of the station as we run to catch up but fall farther
and farther behind, the whistle in the distance, receding
over the mountains. My daughter at four kept asking us to sing,
   Row, Row, Row,
not all that sure herself about the demarcation between dreams and
   waking.
And when we sang to her, Life is but a dream, did she believe us?
When our dog barked at nothing, she asked, Is it barking at a dream?

40

MEDITATION

The blind man stands on his stoop in the rain.
He is old and huge. His hands are bigger
than my head. The rain falls. It falls on him.
He stands there, holding the rail
like someone staring far into the distance.

DRIVING

1.

When I was a kid, this was our way home.
The spreading live oak beside that stock tank
was freighted with familiarity.
Every time returning from the coast,
we took this winding two-lane highway,
saw the tumbled-down rock wall,
that particular hill with huisache trees
at its crown, usually a few cows beneath that live oak,
the fenceline running away toward that distant white steeple.
We took this winding road because it fit us.
It was who we were. It was
like being already home.

2.

Driving the same road last year.
At one point, as I'd always remembered,
the curve of a white caliche road leading away from the highway,
curling along a curving fenceline, mesquite
here and there for shade.
What's so comforting about that road?
At its end, two small frame houses
and a shed. Tree shaded.

The curve bringing you home.
At night perhaps. From a long journey.
From the hospital. From war.
The curving road an encircling arm
drawing you in. Even
if not your home, just one you
drive by now and again.

THESE DAYS

The hot dog vendors let their carts
roll down Thompson St. after sunset
going home. They spit. They whistle.
The windows hang like laundry.
Hunger rules the world.
A woman sweeps the snow,
and three men across the street
are trying on a single shoe.
It belongs to no one. The sidewalks,
the sidewalks are unrelenting.
An old man eats the garbage.
It's the business of survival.
It's the hunger that forces us
to love. The arrow of flying geese
shoots straight through the heart.

SAN ANTONIO

San Antonio is the old woman with cataracts they put on the small hills of the mattress on the back porch. She listens to the banana leaves brushing the screens. She dreams inside her cataracts. She has not much left to say—only "Turn on the fan, Miguel," and "Oh, my bunions." She hears love shuffle through the screen door every night on flat feet. She remembers love that arrived like firemen. "Bombero," she whispers to the shuffling feet. She is becoming roots and branches. She is becoming the stick they beat dogs with.

MULLET

The stupid joy of mullet.
All along the Laguna Madre, mullet
fling themselves into the air for the tiniest sliver
of eternity. Thinking they're flying. Stupid mullet.
Escaping their watery world by three inches, maybe six.
The weight of their tails pulling them back
even as they ascend,
so they never complete an arc,
never cut loose those watery bonds.
The soul of mullet escaping gravity
for a milli-second. And then the dull splash.
Over and over, their short-lived conversions.
All along the Laguna, the plop, plop,
plop of mullet sucked back home.
And again they're at it. As if throwing themselves headlong
up into the abyss. Falling short.
And throwing themselves again. And again the splash.
Their hope and my despair.
The pure illogic of mullet.

A plover flying
watches this. Then skims the surface,
three inches above water, beak open in expectation.
It owns the air. It is the anti-mullet.
A grebe calling, cackling, hooting.
A gull drops headlong

into the water, breaking its glassy plane
on this still day.
Redwing blackbirds, slightly heavier
than a breeze, ride cattails down to the bog.
On shore the cattails are beaten down where alligators bed.
Water, sand, air dissolving into each other
at this convergence of the physical universe.
A place of shifting gravities. And again, plop,
the mullet.

CLEANING FISH

To clean the bullhead,
he took the skin
between his teeth
and stripped it
to the tail. Like
turning a glove
inside out: the
pale hand shivered
and relaxed.

Cleaning bass,
one knife was driven
through the head
as another moved across
the grain: a march
that drove the hopping
scales before it, flecks
glinting like the flashing
backs of small-mouth
moving upstream.

DAN WORKED IN A NURSING HOME

He learned to keep pace
with the old walking backwards
waiting to be born.

THE SEASONS

The woman down the street was born in Prague.
She walks her German police dog by my house every day.
She never smiles. Her clothes are layered thick.
The big dog tugs her toward the alley.
She looks at me blankly as she rounds the pyracantha bushes
and disappears. Her schizophrenic mother never leaves their house.
Crates of imports from the Czech Republic line the driveway.
In some houses it is winter all year long.

I sit here at a stoplight, watching sparrows
whip up the dust from a little mound by the street,
fly up a few inches to bump chests and then drop
again into the dust pile. It's spring.
Across the street a battered yellow Pontiac pulls up to the curb.
A woman in a green housedress, pillows of fat
spilling out, opens the car door
and climbs out the driver's side
as a round man in khakis exits the passenger side.
They meet behind the Pontiac
in an undulating embrace.
Then they slide back into the Pontiac
and drive away.

IT CAN'T BE DENIED

Life is larger than any two people combined.
Life is larger than two people. Three even,
even if you put them front to front
and front to back. Life is bigger than that.
I walk around the city. I see so many people
step over each other. People lie in the street.
People lean out of windows on the pillows
they're airing. And there are people hiding
in apartments. And two children who sit together
on a stoop and do not speak. And a woman
gets up from her chair and walks back into a shadow.
Life is bigger than all of them. You can count them:
One man ties his shoe. One man eats his supper
behind a café window. Count them: a woman
stops at a corner and turns around. A girl
hangs by her knees from a railing. See—
adding and subtracting, multiplying even,
but still not life. This one and that one
and that one. The subways are filled. The doors slide open.
No one leaves the train. The skyscrapers sag. There is a face
at every window and where there are no windows,
there is a face. I could go on forever. The stands fill up.
The people are shouting. No one goes home. At this corner,
at that corner, crowds wait for the signals to change.
The traffic moves. The traffic stops moving.
Inside the buses lights go on.

LIGHT YEARS

Dogs eat the garbage.
The streets never move.
What the day takes
the night gives back.
I am constantly here.
The pavement. The sidewalks.
The stone steps.
No refuge.
No corner human enough.
Stars long dead
bore their way through the darkness.
Windows climb the night.
No relief.
Someone is always going to work.
Men emerge from the subway.
Their black gloves,
dark lunch pails. The echo
of their footsteps drowns
whatever they are saying.

THANKSGIVING

The sky draining off at sunset.
Under so much beauty, there is so much beauty.
Under an orange sky a woman is waiting for the bus.
She has little red lips painted on big brown lips.
When the headlights hit them, you see them.
Suddenly, the world is inside me.

THE CALCULUS
OF FALLING BODIES

THE CALCULUS OF FALLING BODIES

Who carries the black bean? The accountant
prays in coach so the plane won't fall,
a black smudge flowering on his prostate.
The used-car salesman jogs blocks each night,
never smokes, cuts deals with God, steps
off a curb into the grillwork of a Buick.
Looking the wrong way. I was told
what you fear will kill you. But there's too much
to choose from. One of them will get me, sure.
Mortality has all the options, compared
to my one. Some day it will arrive like a terrible wind
admired from a great distance. The storm
beautiful across the desert valley
until the downdraft hits, flattening
the huisache branch where the red tanager
had just been riding, lighting up
the evening like a rose.

HARVEST

A girl in Bangladesh puts down her scythe
and walks away from the harvest.
A doctor in the minor emergency clinic
cuts the thread of his last stitch with his teeth
and goes home to write poetry.

I could get up from this desk, this computer,
this window overlooking the gray parking lot,
and walk out into the light mist I've been watching
all morning. A wet stain grows
on the concrete wall across the lot

and a few mulberry leaves hang over its top
heavy with rain. I could drop my scythe
and walk out into the mist, past the concrete walls,
into the trees, and keep walking
away from a harvest slowly diminishing.

LOSING UNCLE ED

Out the screen door
of the ranch house weathered Uncle Ed
one day passed into the lake,
fishing pole and tackle box in hand.
This time he did not stop,
as he always had, at the water's edge
beneath the cottonwood. This time
his slow, sure mule-step took him
past the rowboat pulled up on the sand,
past the drying seine. This time
he waded in through water at his knees,
through lily pads, to reeds
and water at his waist, and moved on.
          "I choke with water at my waist,"
he once told me, his hand
around his throat. "When I was a boy,
Nate pulled me from the Dnepr
when sailors threw me in."
He passed through water
at his chest and at his neck;
he passed beneath the trotline
he had strung years ago.
He went under, fishing pole in hand.

Now he walks among strange faces,
his thoughts washing like the moss.
He is fishing for some clue
to the sudden change in atmosphere,
to the murky understanding that surrounds him.
He is wandering, pole in hand,
with the large-mouth bass, the sun perch,
awaiting Nate's saving grip.
He moves with the catfish
along the bottom
into the deepest pools.

SHAKING HANDS

All I can do is touch
your skin, almost water,
almost dead, and hear
the bubbles popping in your mouth,
while a cold spring breaks
into your brain. Your eyes
swim like blindfish in the light.

When I shake your hand
I feel I'm the anchor
you are trying desperately
to lift.

HYGIENE

The nurses in flowered smocks and running shoes
laugh as they emerge from the hospital and head
for the sunlit café where they sit around a table,
removing their sneakers and fixing their hair.
How can they be laughing with a world of pustules,
fractured limbs, paralyzing fear and stony death
just behind them? Or are they laughing

at the bodies they've worked on, like mine
undressing behind a sheet in the ice-cold emergency room,
its hard steel surfaces and unrelenting light.
Even while pondering my own mortality, I was overwhelmed
by the robust nurses, serenely physical in a sea
of vulnerable flesh, whose job is touching
the skin and all it leads to. So that

even undressing in the emergency room as the nurse
looked the other way, even while waiting to be told
my fate, I found myself tiptoeing
the short eggshell walk between humiliation and desire.
My mind darting like minnows (not leaping like dolphins),
like minnows swimming to stay even
as the world rushes past going the other way.

No time to contemplate dying in the abstract
with the echo of earlier pain still cruising my chest cavity,
tape sticking to chest, back, shoulders, ankles.
Held down by wires to machines
and my own nakedness.
But nothing is abstract about nurses in sunlight,
their rubber-soled forthrightness and easy laughter,
as if they're the onrushing water, and sickness
and death are bends in the river, the high
and low places that shape the stream.

WAR IS A CURE FOR LONELINESS

War is a cure for loneliness. Like football. Crush each other.
Share sweat, spit, blood. O Band of Brothers. Sitting on benches
among islands of damp towels on the locker room floor.
Waiting for the beads to stop streaming down your chest.
Together. Death is another cure. Not war played out on black
screens, red dots standing for targets, standing for people,
dashes slowly arcing until they meet the red dots,
standing for people, and erase them. But war
walked down dark alleys at night. Fear erasing loneliness.
        Band of Brothers.
Boots crunching gravel ahead of you, behind you. The crunch
        displacing love.
Ready to engage. Sex can cure loneliness. Sometimes.
Night vision. Boots crunching. The world is infrared. Talk to me.
Talk to me. Conversations over dinner. You with your screen.
Me with mine. What we post is who we are. Ready to engage.
Tapping to each other on keys from cubicles. A muted cry to leap
the gray, carpeted walls. You can live on Facebook for months
after you die. Meaning is a cure for loneliness. Nations are lonely.
War has meaning. Until it no longer does. This pixelated life. Touch me.
Touch me. Ferry me across a sea of hands,
endlessly.
        Walk down a forest path.
Pink azaleas in bloom. Blue jays squawking, dancing with each other,
fifteen feet apart, branch to branch, tree to tree. Dung beetles
roll their Sisyphean balls at the edge of the path.

Break open old milkweed pods. The white wings
feather into the breeze and lift. They slowly float away.
Alone in the woods and embraced.

AT 51

I'm glad my losses are gradual.
We outlive all our joys. But
just now I've been dancing on the front porch
with my beautiful daughters as they gyrate
down the uncut trails of their green lives.
Even the setting sun seems to pause
before it drops.

AN ENDING

His dying fills at most a room
where I sit beside his swollen hand,
opening and closing, catching
and releasing wings of light.
His dying moves into him
from where it stood inside the door,
beside the window looking out.
And I move closer, lay a finger
where his elbow bends,
keep within his last perceiving.
His eye gives up its light to me,
and I sit against the turning skin
inside a dream he's carrying to sleep.

THINGS ARE GONNA BREAK

for my father

Tonight I picked up a novel I'd left half-finished some time ago.
And when I opened to the place marker, I found
it was from the lodge in Red River where we'd stayed
three nights before you died. That is,
you were alive the last time I was reading this book
on the front porch of our cabin among the redwoods
across from the stocked trout pond and not far from the narrow
Red River, where we could hear the faint tingling of bells
inside the rushing water while girls screaming with delight
were swinging high into the trees on boards hung from lower
                redwood branches.

I'm sure you were worrying about something,
probably about us up there without a telephone.
It was three days before that kid, reaching for his milk
while driving too fast, plowed into you
on your morning route to work, in the middle
of the left turn you always took, the end of consciousness
drained away on the white curb by the thick green grass
and the house I must have passed every day for 18 years
growing up. I keep thinking, after opening this book,
what if we'd come home one day early, cut it short a day?

What if we'd driven straight through, stopped by your house
for the night, made you 30 seconds later for work the next morning

by mentioning a box score or talking about the weather?
What if, instead of opening this book on the front porch of that cabin,
I'd gone inside and said, I've had enough, let's go home?
I know it's the stuff of bad movies, but
what if I'd gotten sick or restless and we'd packed up the car
and headed home, not stopping in the Davis Mountains for that one day,
that day driving down a mountain, when I'd felt a terror grab hold of me
like I'd never felt before? When I felt I'd lost all control.

I was almost paralyzed with fear, certain
that my brakes would give way, wondering
how to steer my family safely down the winding road,
not knowing what this cloud was that had descended
so completely around me that my children became terrified.
What were you worrying about that night?
We could have been there in your kitchen,
throwing off the timing of this dark universe,
talking about the pennant race and what you thought
was my aimlessness, though we never talked about that directly.

It almost sucked me under. It scared the girls,
the fear that shook me. I didn't know it was you.
Your last hours were probably spent
trying to tune into the Astros game on the radio
while reading a book and drowning out the worrisome noise of life.
This is more than idle speculation. More than regret.
This is the two girls swinging high in the redwoods,
one shouting to the other, "It takes my stomach away.
And I feel like I'm gonna fall
and things are gonna break."

68

FOR MY FATHER

No ceremony else?
          —Hamlet

1.

After the good memorial, after the measured eulogies,
the kaddish, the rational grief, the delicately apportioned sadness,
after the assessment, sum and total, of a good man,
the hushed, polite exchanges, the averted glances,
firm handshakes, muscled hugs, muffled discussions
over teacakes and honeyed ham as the great-nieces and nephews run
among card tables piled with salads and cakes, the dishes
continuously washed and put away by dutiful cousins
who don't know what else to do, after the door closes
behind the last funeral guest, and we take off our shoes,
comes the dark.

Comes irrational grief. Comes absence, the hollow
that haunts this house, these rooms, this lonely sitting
in the living room in our socks. Come distances
unmeasured and immeasurable. Comes time rolled back
again and again. To last Thursday, when he was alive.
To the phone call, just Sunday a week, when he said
he couldn't wait to see us. To Tuesday morning when
he got into his car and left the house forever. Come his sad eyes,
his smile, not in this room but in some middle distance,
there and not there, transparent as it hovers in the mind.

69

Give me keening. Give me wailing. The high-pitched, unending
ululation of Berber misery. Give me ancient pounding grief.
Drunken Irish fury. Lashing and moaning
by the funeral pyre. Rhythmic, ritual sobbing.
Not carefully circumscribed chaos, the gaping hole
surrounded by flower gardens. Give me rocking
and rocking a thousand times in prayer. A thousand more.
Touch the prayer shawl to the coffin, kiss it, touch it again
and again. The physical separation. The earth-tearing,
        heart-wrenching break.

Torn from its moorings, the ship drags us out to sea.
And when we can stand no more,
we let go.

2.

Then the dust to be scattered. Under a sheltering live oak
whose shade he often found. This dust of him.
Holding him in a box. Feeling him shift, grain against grain.
This ultimate weight. Where's his breath in this?
His lips? His long slender legs that used to lie on the floor
next to my bed when some strange noise riffled the banana leaves?
Where are they? Which handful of dust? His laugh?
Which part his sad eyes, seeming to wait for this moment always?
Which part his hands? Here?
Or here? Mixing with the South Texas clay.
Blowing in the hot August breeze. Where is he?
Ululululululululululululululululu.

A WALK IN THE PARK

I mean like here we're on the beach worrying about a party
and they're over there fighting a war. It's weird to think about.
　　　　　—Girl interviewed on NPR, March 20, 2003

Screech owls high in an elm. Mustard green
blossoms hanging from elm branches this spring
evening. As I walk through the park, the thump
thump of a slow dribble on cement
as fathers play ball while their toddlers swing,
watched by big sisters, who themselves pump
their legs to soar into the purpling sky
just before sunset. Crisp March air.
The gray fox I'd seen here once before
wanders out of the underbrush, gives me the eye
and dives back toward its lair
among the dark green leaves along the creek shore.

At that moment, I'd guess the bombs began.
At that moment, some kid was pissing in his pants
in a sand-caked tent in Kuwait with the dogs unleashed.
Our own nature turned loose, to be feared now more than
Nature's elements—earthquakes, the syncopated dance
of a tornado across a sleeping town. No match for the beast
inside us. The screech owl's elegiac call
is almost quaint. The gray fox a relic of some ancient world
that not so long ago we knew.

71

Is it left behind forever? Was it so great a fall,
so faint a memory, turned tail and run back into the wood?
Fox, take me with you
down among the lichen-covered rocks, the mossy berm,
damp holes where you wait out the storm above the flood.
Below radar screens, missile intelligence, buzz bombs,
to a place raging waters rush like blood.

NO END

There is no end to life.
No end to anything.
You walk east
and the buildings fall on top of each other.
The world gives way. And still a dog wanders up,
a rat, a boy holding his pants.
No end, you see.
There's no hope. Everywhere you look—
life clinging to life.
I wander to the ends of the island,
to the last rotting board of the last rotting pier,
and find mollusks hanging on.
Even when there's no reason for it,
life continues. It has no limits.
There's no place life turns around and says,
Beyond this is intolerable.
This is as far as it goes.

WHAT IS IT?

It's not the blood. The blood that seeps
into the bag running from his single kidney,
the bag duct-taped shut as my friend's brother walks
the last months, weeks, days of his life
from room to room. It's not the blood.
It's not the pain. The anxiety?
The sweat-soaked nights? What is it
that makes the difference between now and when he's gone?
So slight a difference if you're only looking
at what's breaking down and its end.
The wheels come off, the parts laid out.
Crumbling before your eyes. Just a hair's breadth
from gone. But that's not it: that hair.
Still the huge chasm between now and later.
Between him and not him. Between walking, thinking,
waking, talking and not. What is it?
The time he now spends smoking in the garage
among his tools? Is it smoking and thinking?
Is it almost laughing? Is it walking among family
as still more than a memory? Is that it?

Or is it my Aunt Helen, climbing out of a coma
and, only hours before her death, asking
for her makeup—powder, lipstick, eyeliner,
rouge for her cheeks? So that amid the tangle
of tubes and oxygen masks we would still see her

as she chose to be seen,
we would recognize her as she knew herself,
so we would know that in the antiseptic, unfamiliar stillness
of that hospital room, in the presence of a body all played out,
she was still there,
she was still there.

Or is it my neighbor Cruz? Left eye gone
to diabetes. One organ after another on the verge
of collapse. You hear him coming from blocks away,
fighting his latest used truck up the hill,
pushing and grinding his way home. He goes through one
old pickup after another, pushing it farther
than it was meant to go, driving it into the ground,
the parts of each rescued to feed the next.

Or is it this? A woman in Chalmers Courts
has the taxi stop halfway up the hill.
The driver puts her wheelchair in the middle of Comal St.
and ceremoniously swings the door open
as she disembarks into the chair. She has one leg.
And with a push
of that single foot she hurtles backward
down the hill, steering by memory
in a wide flamboyant arc,
gaining speed to swing
at the last instant into the driveway of the courts
and up over a hump, still pushing
with her one foot up the hill until she's home.

Then she waves to the cabbie
who has stopped to watch her art.
Is that it? Pushing, bumping backwards to home.
Is that it? Up the hill. Up the hill.
Is that it? The I am, I am, I am.

THE ART OF POETRY

Ain't it a shame, he said, meaning the two women there
walking on the curb as he brought the truck around a corner,
meaning they were young, their dark hair caught the light,
and he was married and I was soon to be, and for us
they came too late walking on that curb. And another time
he said, Ain't it a shame, meaning for all my education,
I could not back a trailer through a gate to be unloaded,
couldn't cut a straight line with a torch,
couldn't load steel pipe for hours with the August sun
          in Texas hanging on me,
could never know the years he spent drifting full-muscled
          into manhood.

The world is so peculiar. In the pipeyard
under the caliche is the black dirt
and under the black dirt is the limestone that holds the water
          they are always drilling for
and under the water somewhere deep is burning rock, meaning
that what we need is always just beyond us,
meaning that so much of our own lives is just beyond us.

And by the pipeyard runs the highway
that also runs by my grandfather and Uncle Ed
where they are buried in the black dirt
just where Uncle Ed used to wander when he got old,
walking to the pipeyard in his sleep.

Ain't it a shame. Even the great thoughts are just beyond us,
not that far off, just through the dirt somewhere,
just rattling in the mesquite. You see, my father wrote poetry
where the trucks lifted the caliche dust
that settled on the cold black steel.
Nothing is too far away that it can't almost be summoned back,
even the lost thoughts of the living,
even the dead thoughts of the dead. Out of reach
but not so far. Ain't it a shame.
The ghosts almost come alive.

ACKNOWLEDGMENTS

Some of these poems have appeared previously in the following journals: *Borderlands 14, Borderlands 19, Borderlands 26, Indiana Writes 2, Texas Observer,* and *Texas Poetry Calendar 2015.*

"Work" appeared in *What Have You Lost?* (Greenwillow Books, 2001). "Mullet" appeared in *Is This Forever, or What?* (Greenwillow Books, 2004).

ABOUT THE AUTHOR

Geoff Rips was born and raised in San Antonio, Texas. He is a former editor of the *Texas Observer* and has been a Soros Open Society Institute Fellow. He worked as the Freedom-to-Write Committee coordinator for PEN American Center and was the principal author of its report, *UnAmerican Activities* (City Lights Books, 1981). His 2008 novel, *The Truth*, received the AWP (Association of Writers & Writing Programs) Award for the Novel. Rips has worked with community organizations along the Texas/Mexico border to bring water and wastewater services to border colonias. He currently works for Texas Rio Grande Legal Aid. He is a member of the Texas Institute of Letters and PEN American Center and has published poetry, fiction and journalism in various journals and newspapers over the years. He lives in Austin, Texas, with his wife, Nancy Maniscalco. They have two daughters, Gabriela and Sascha.